Amazing World Of Dogs Adult Coloring Book

This book belongs to:

____

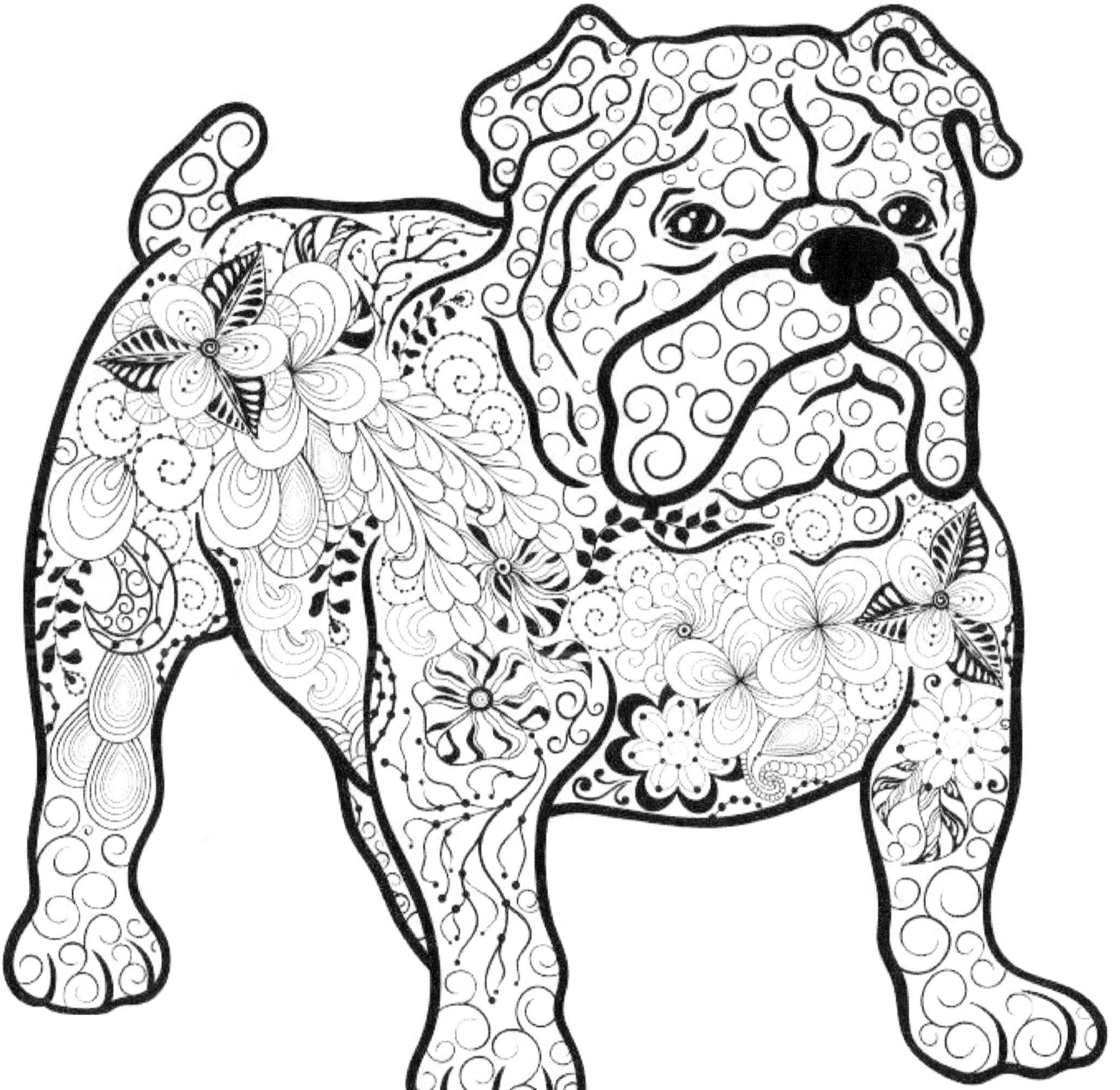

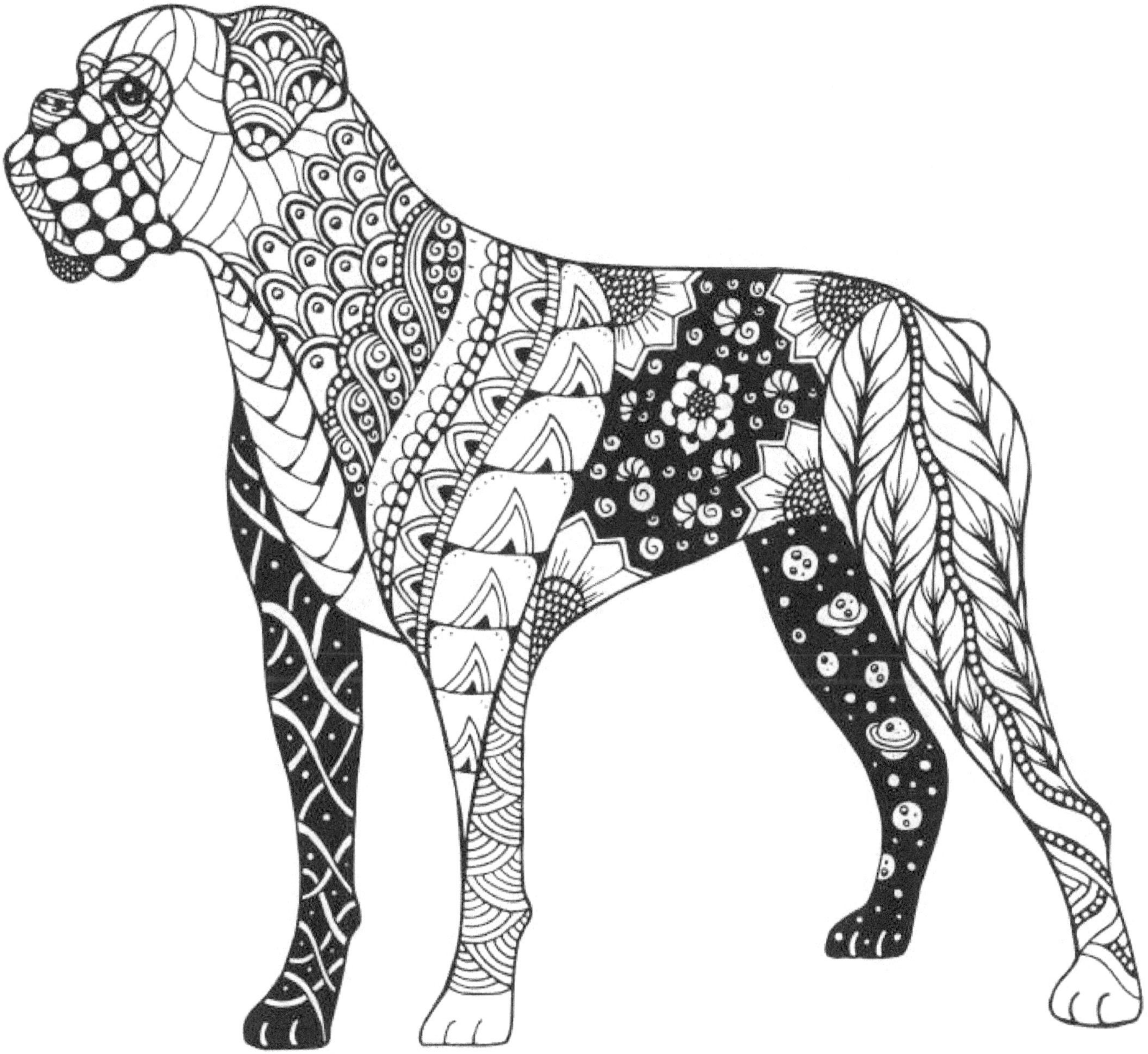

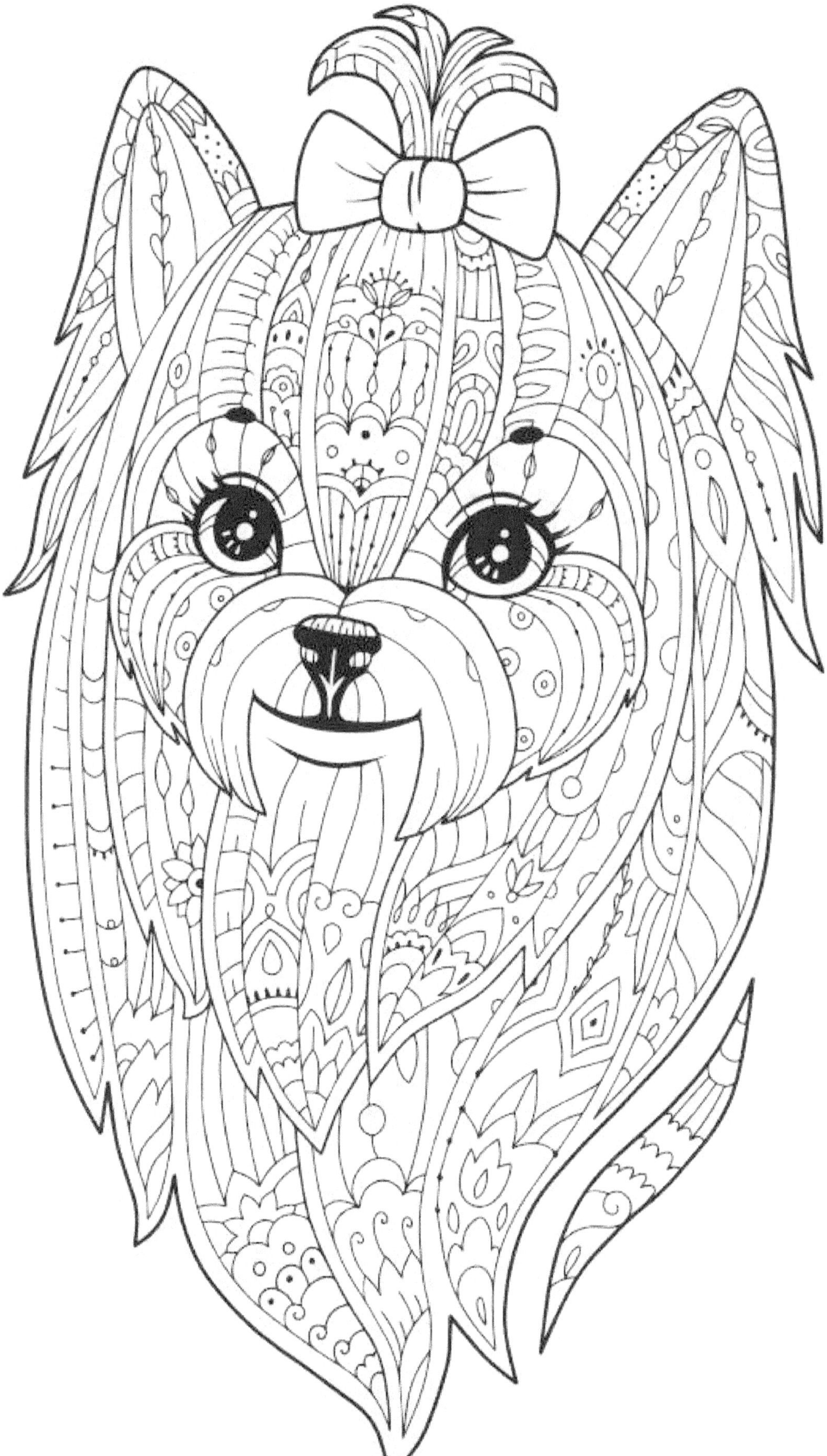

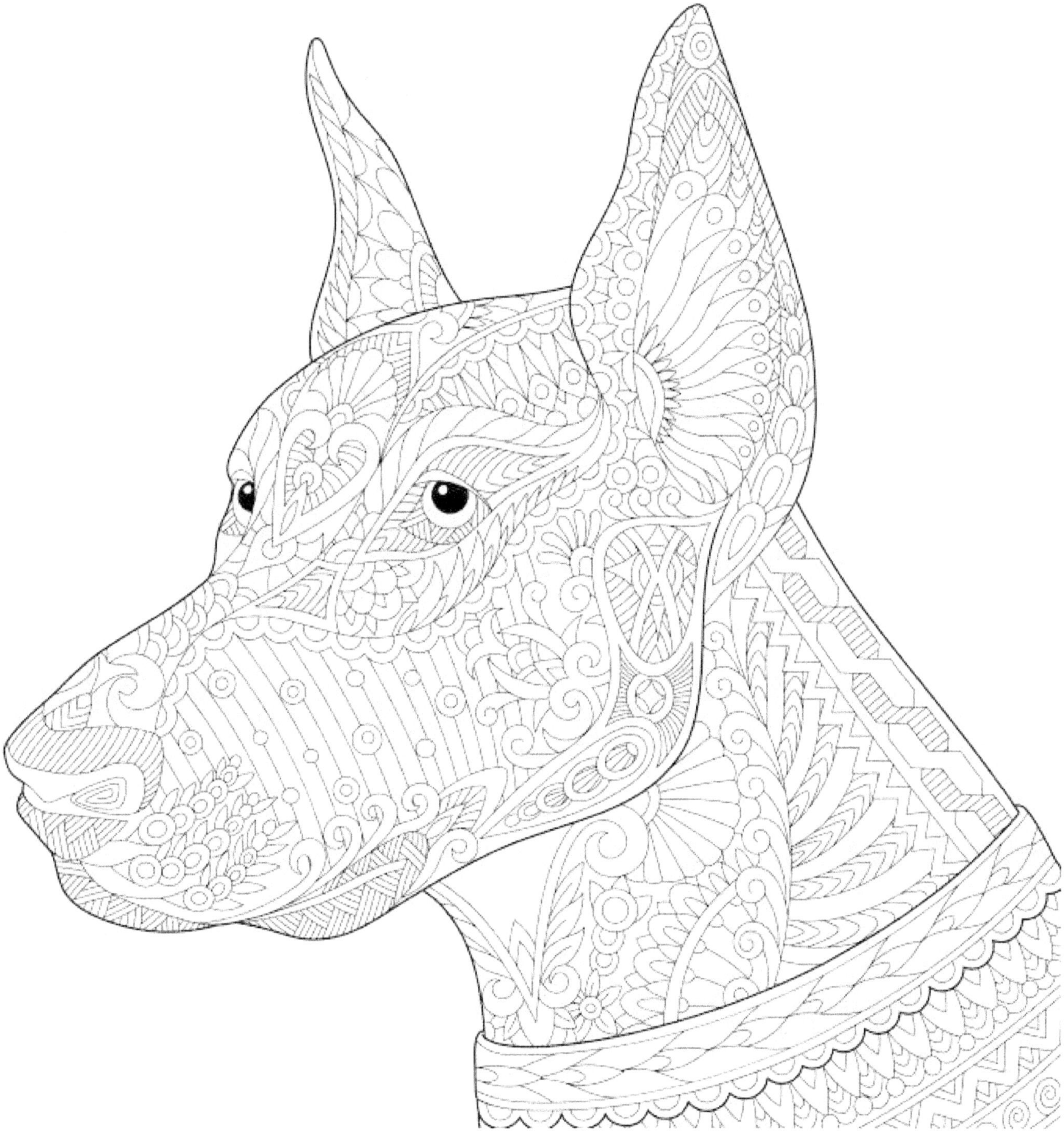

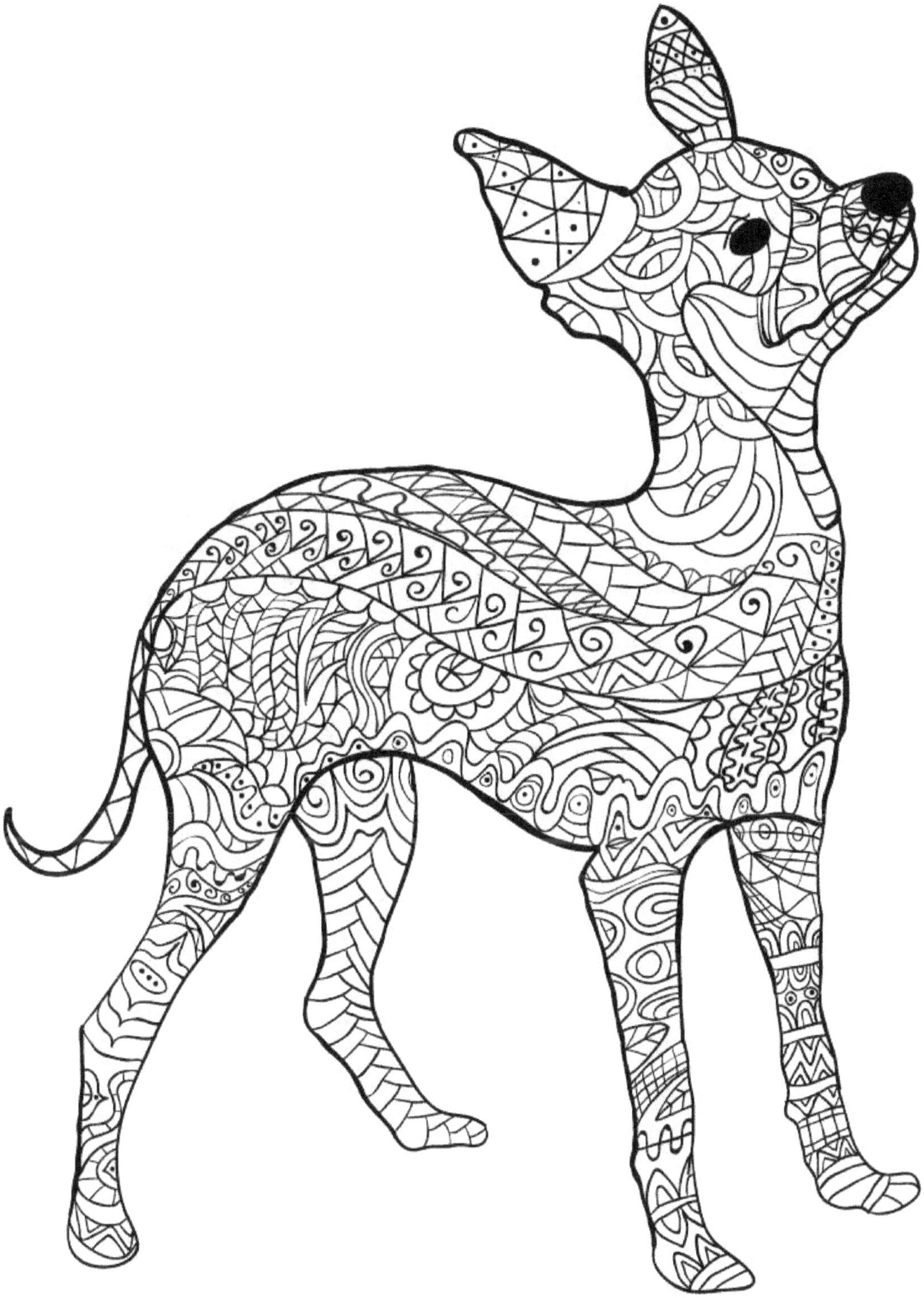

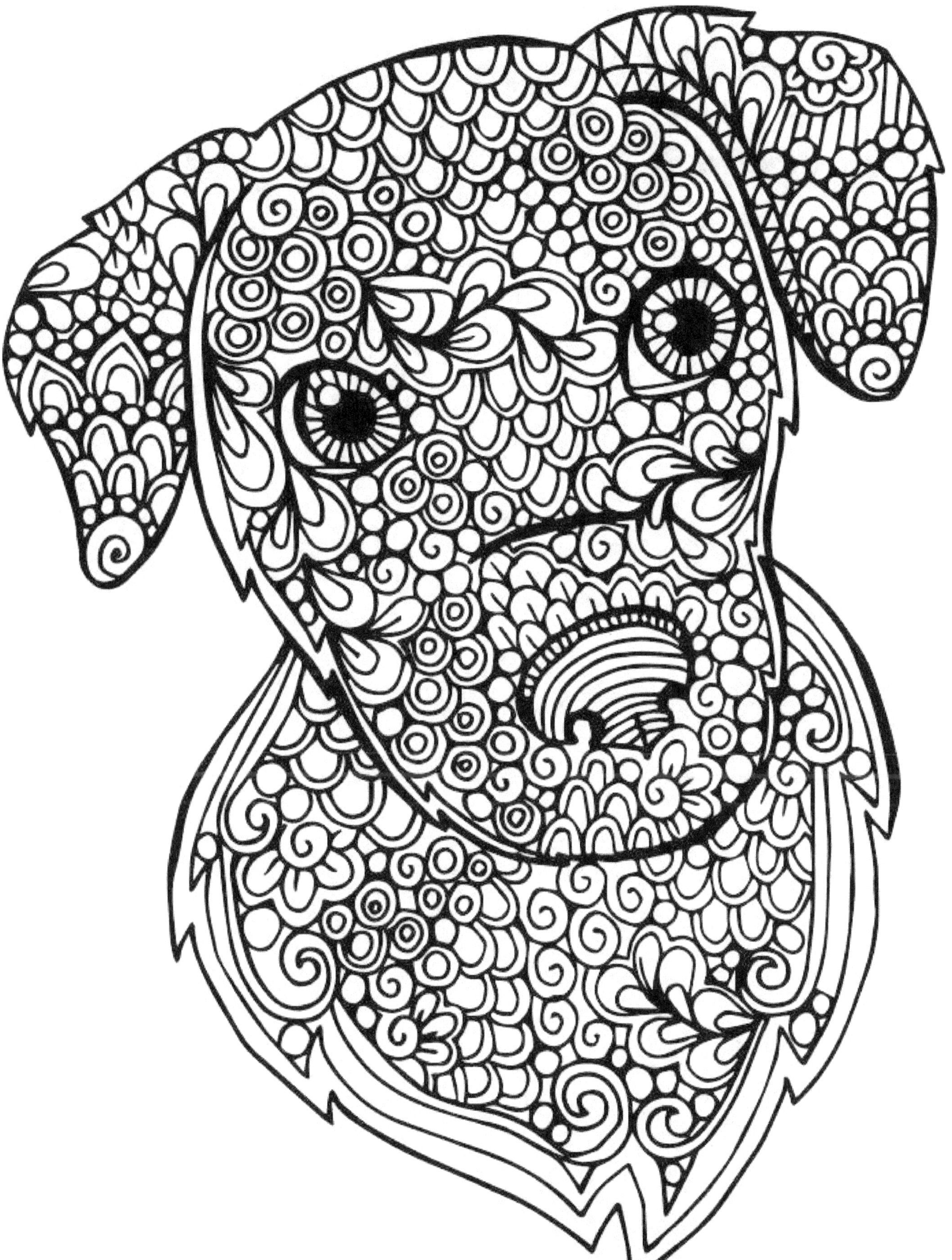

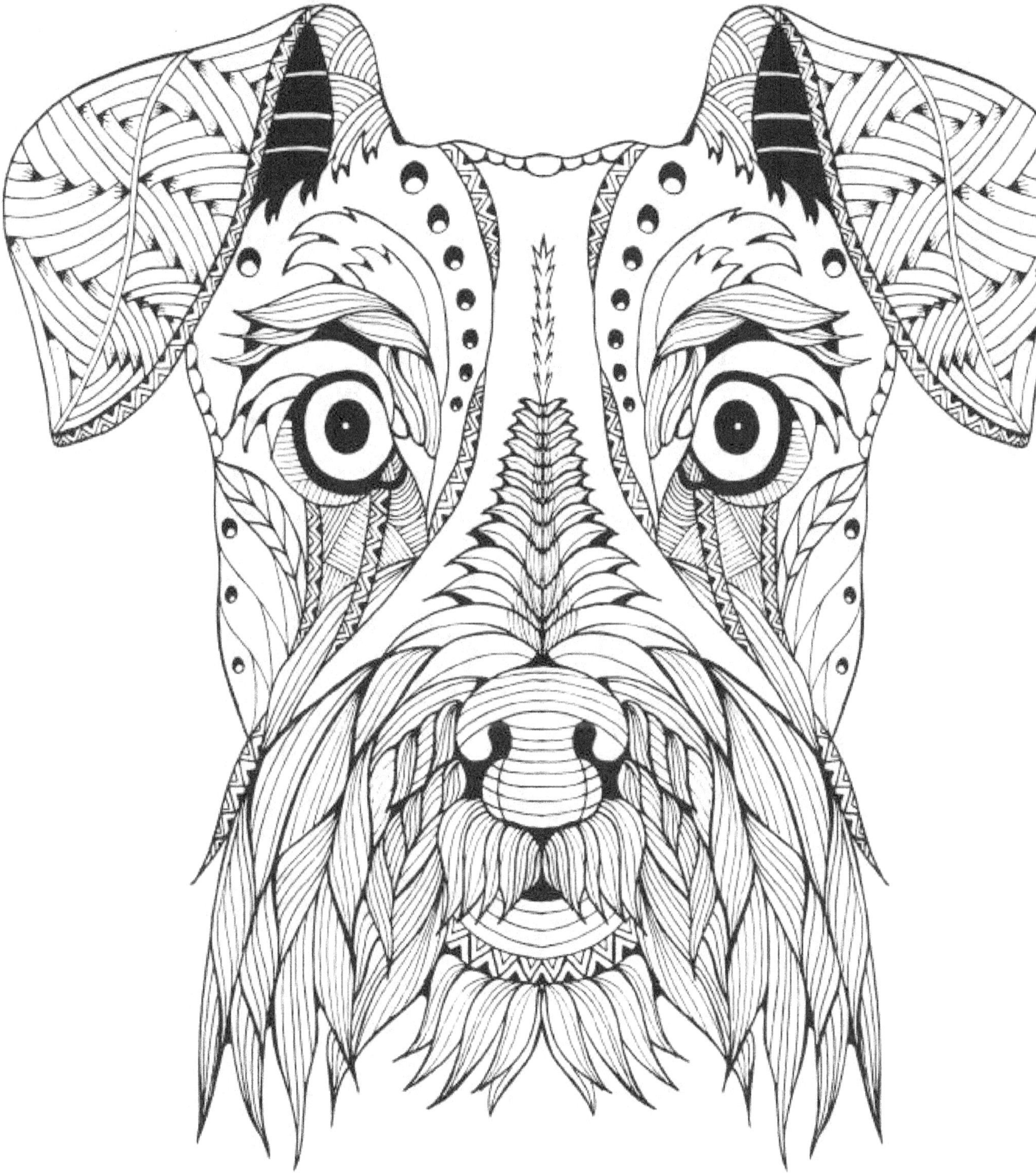

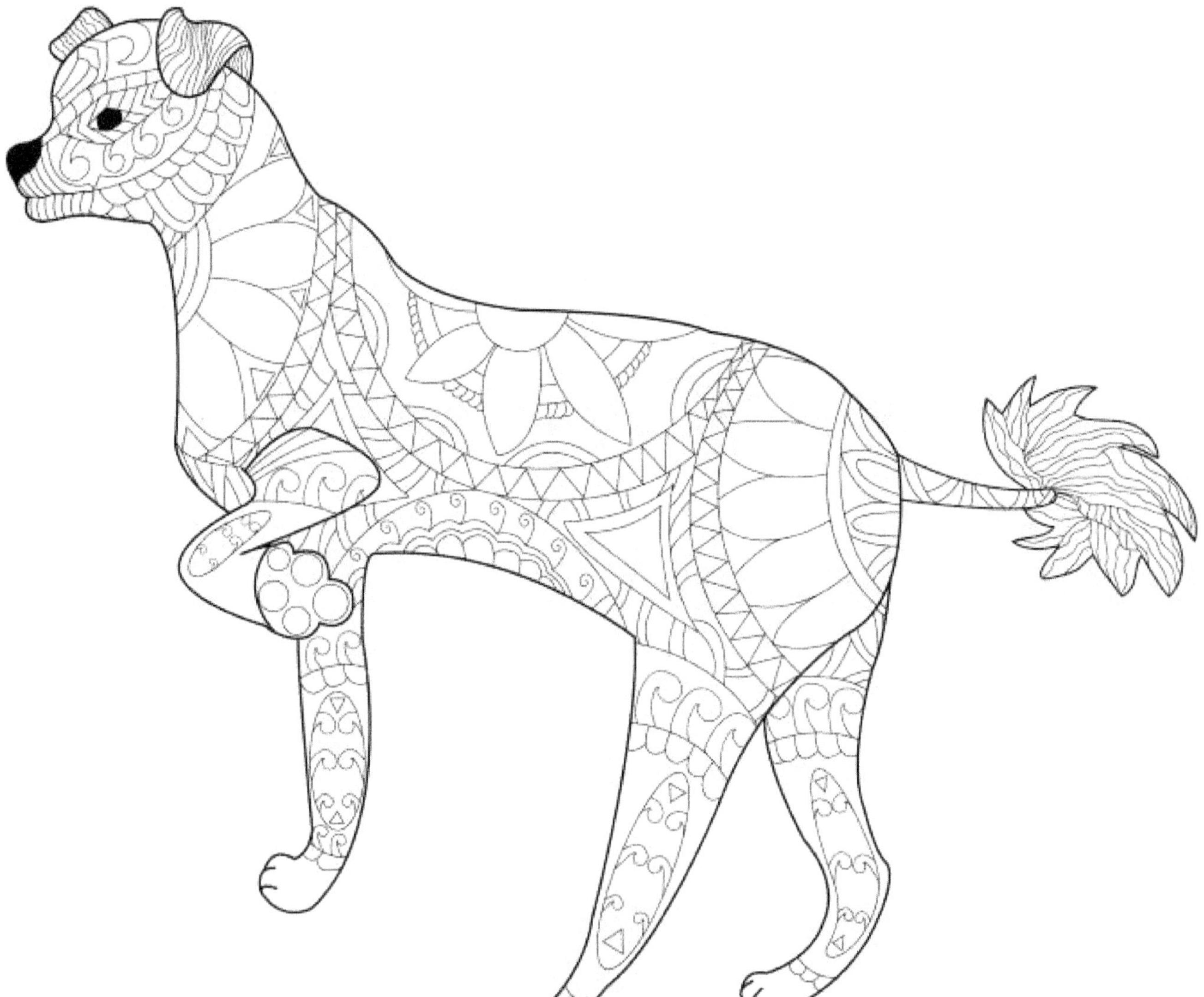

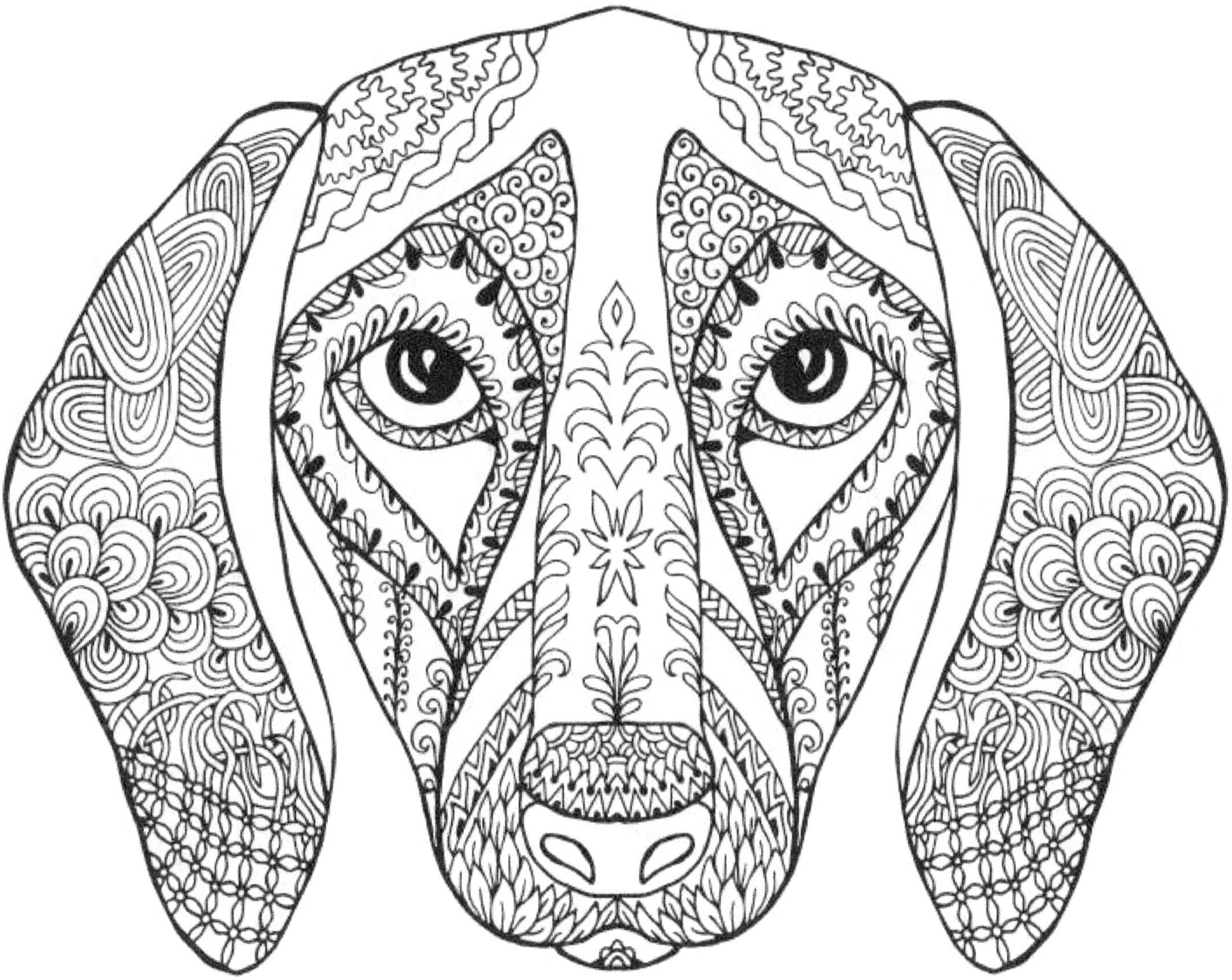

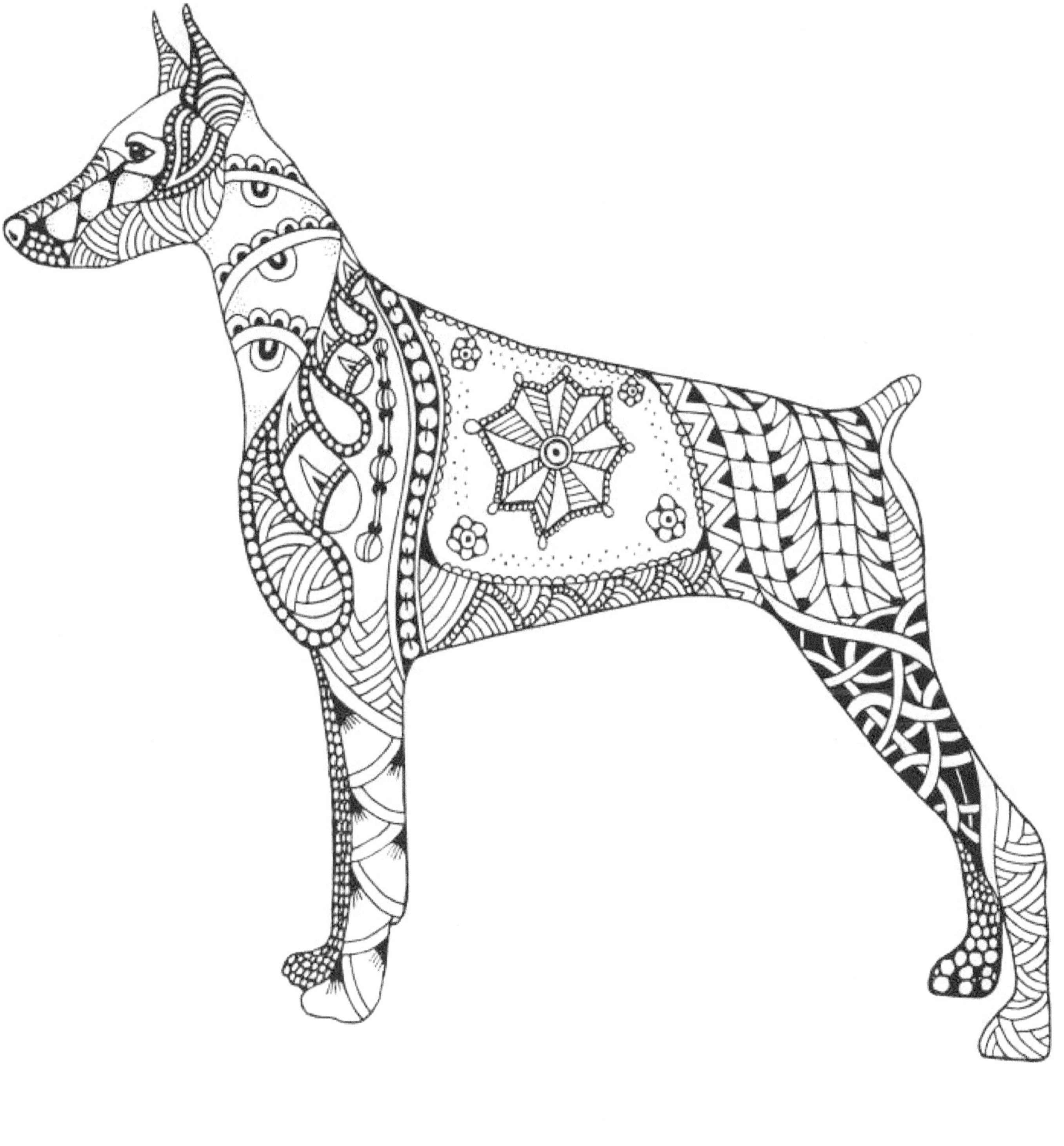

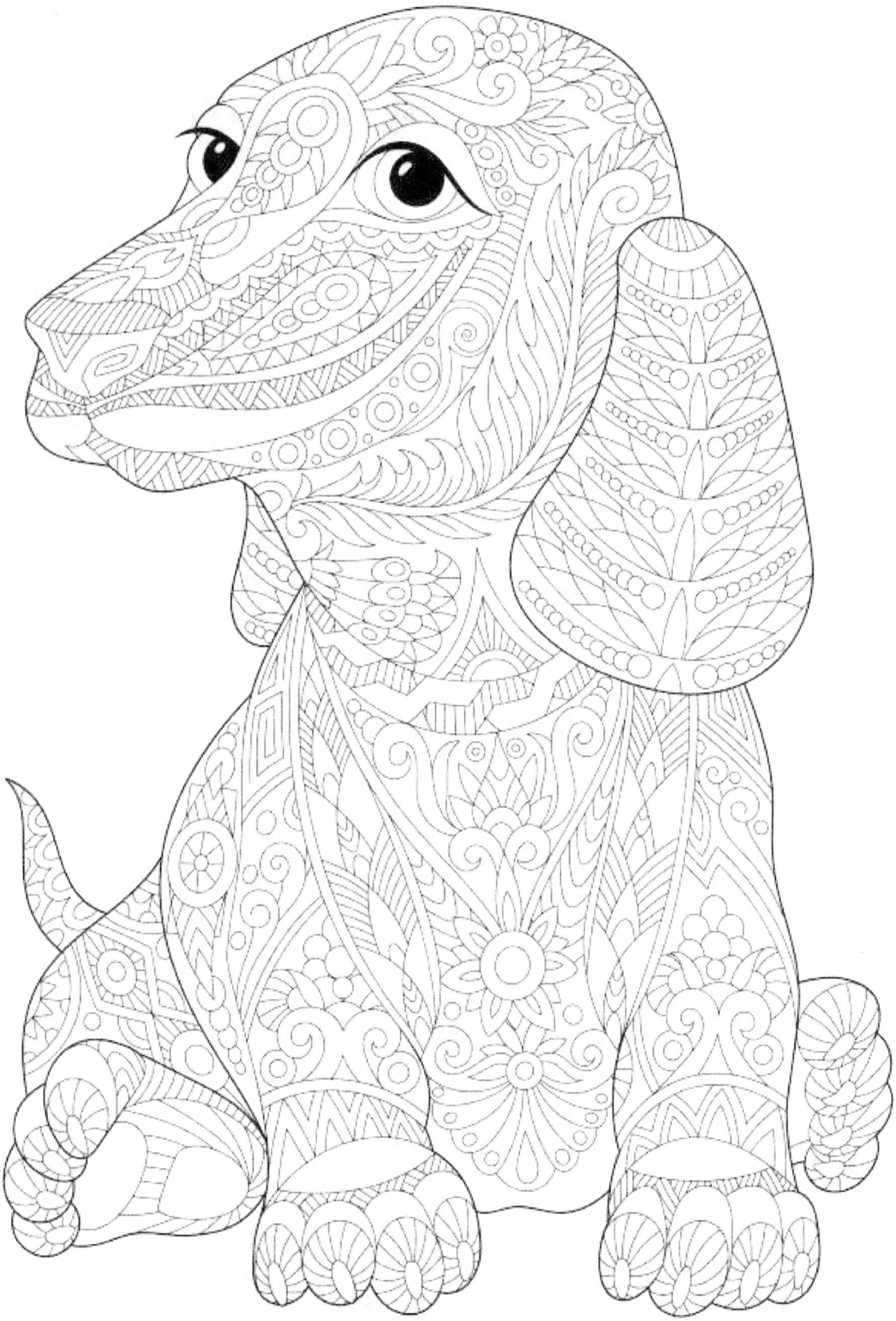

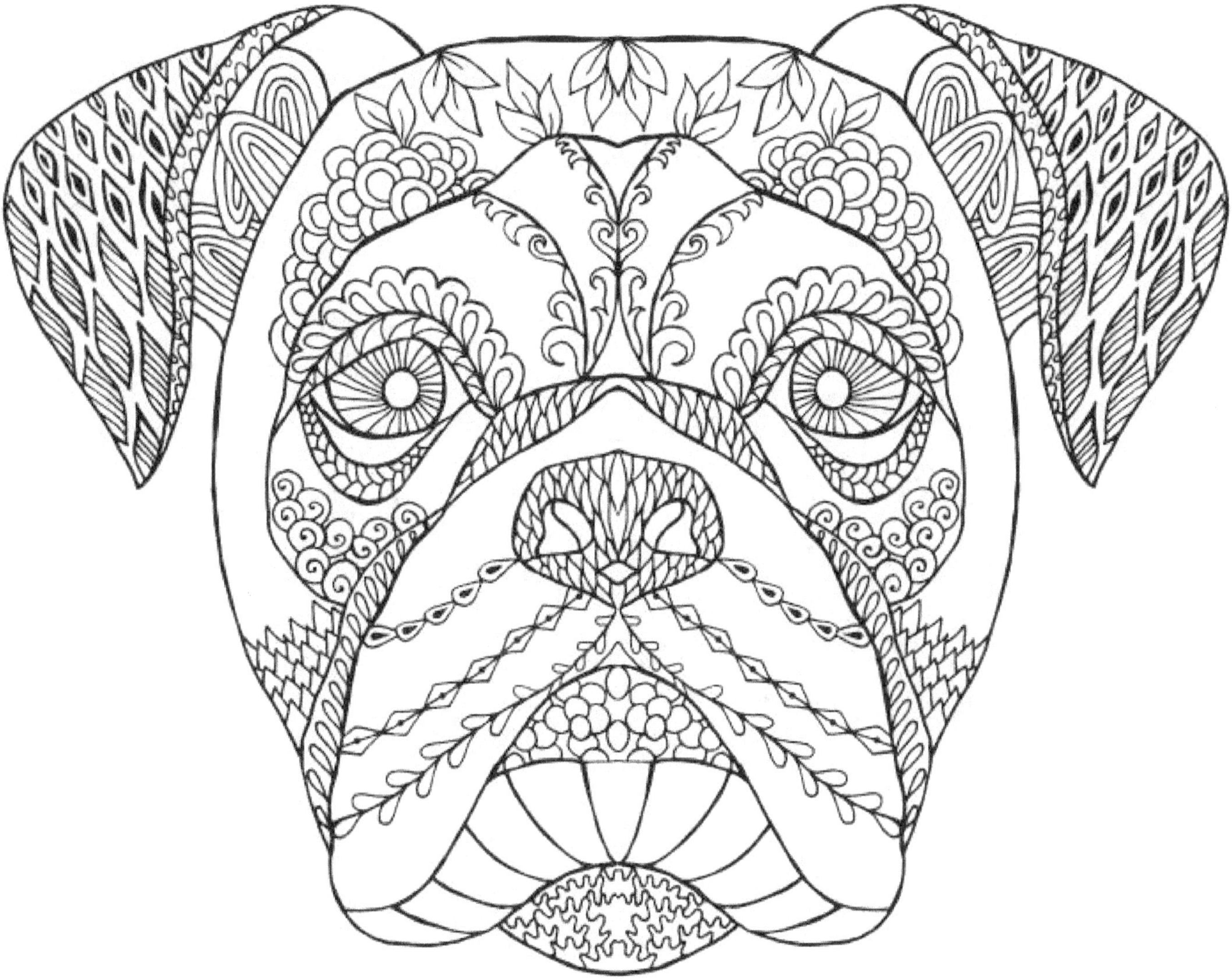

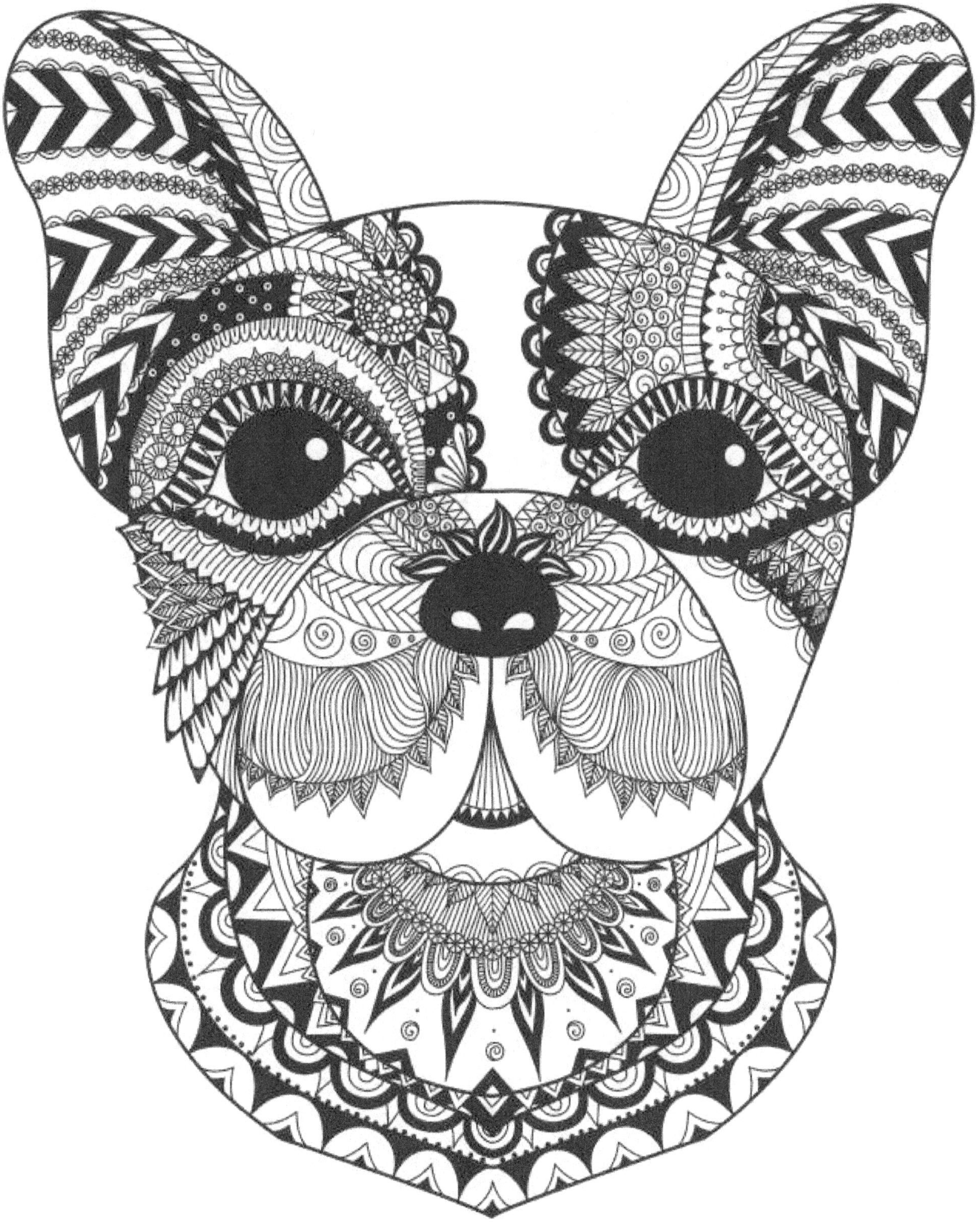

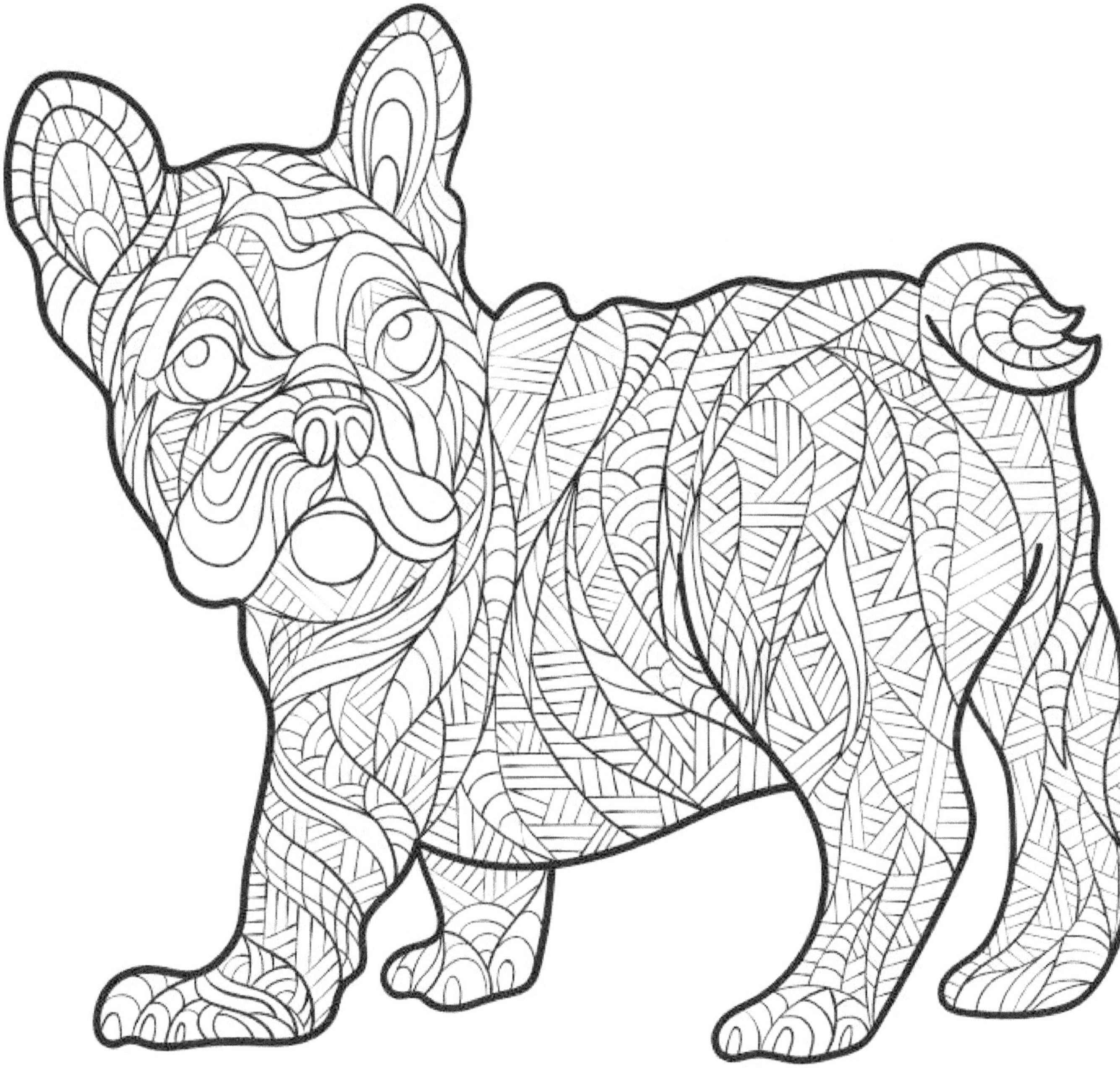

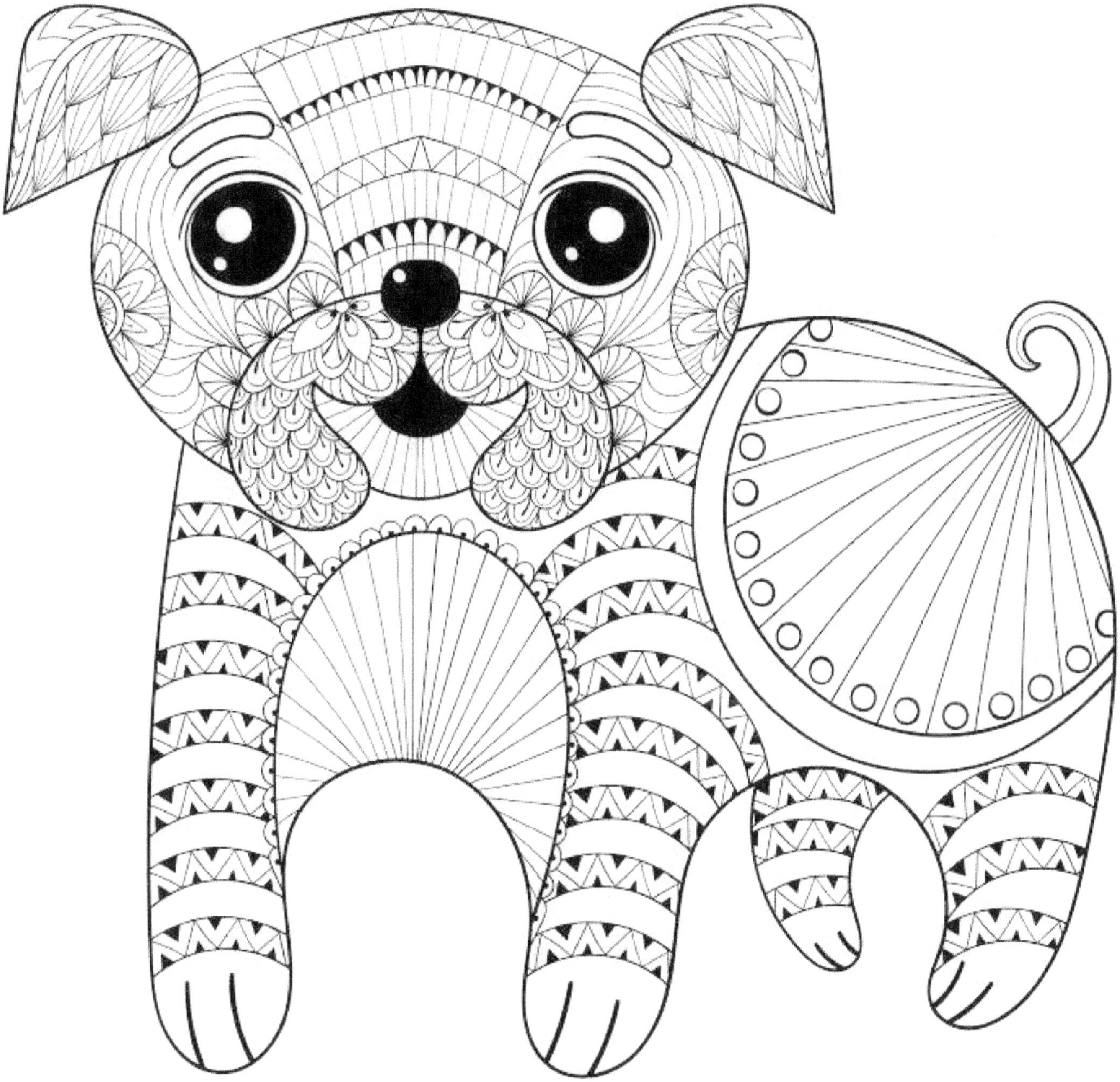

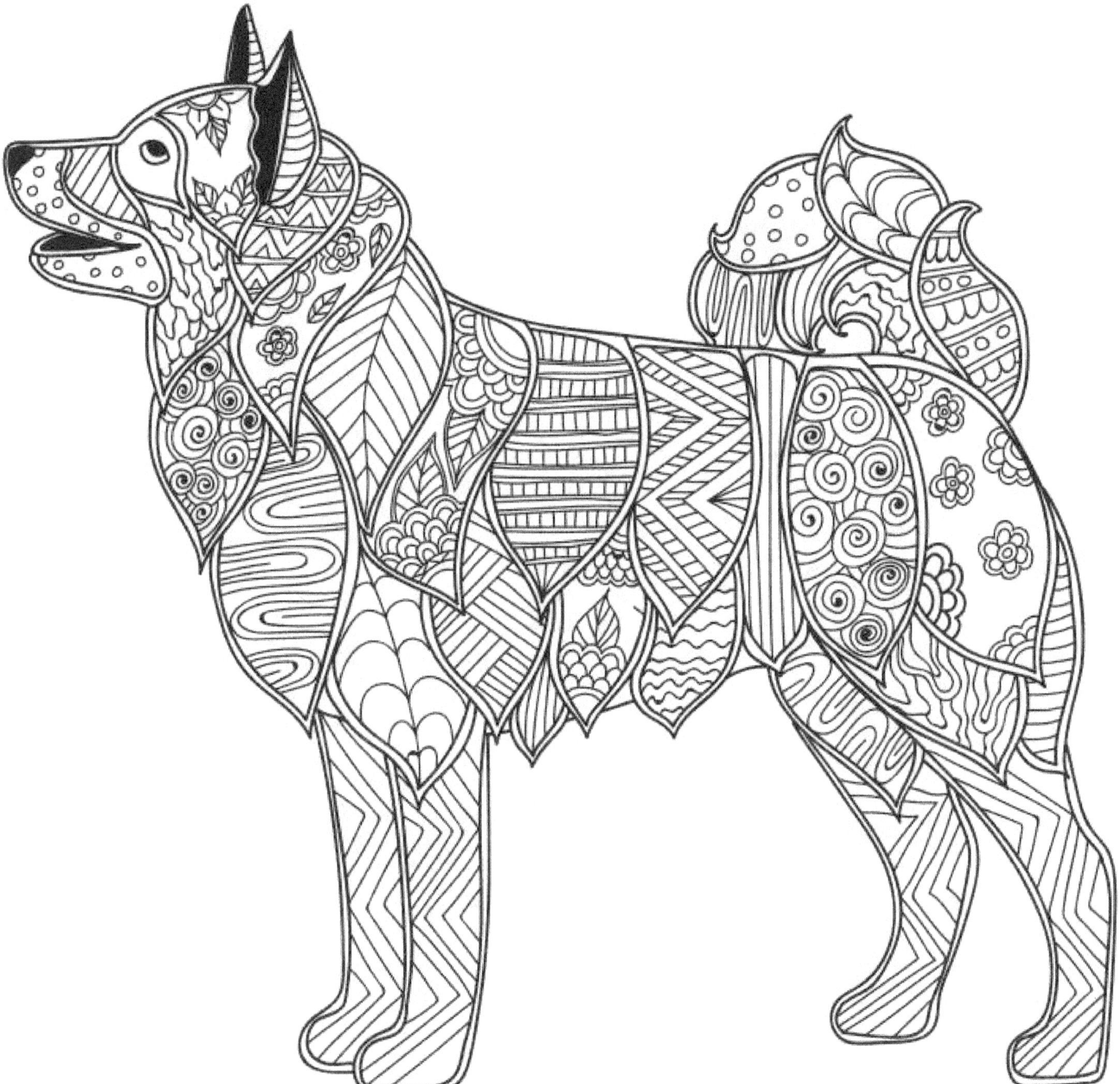

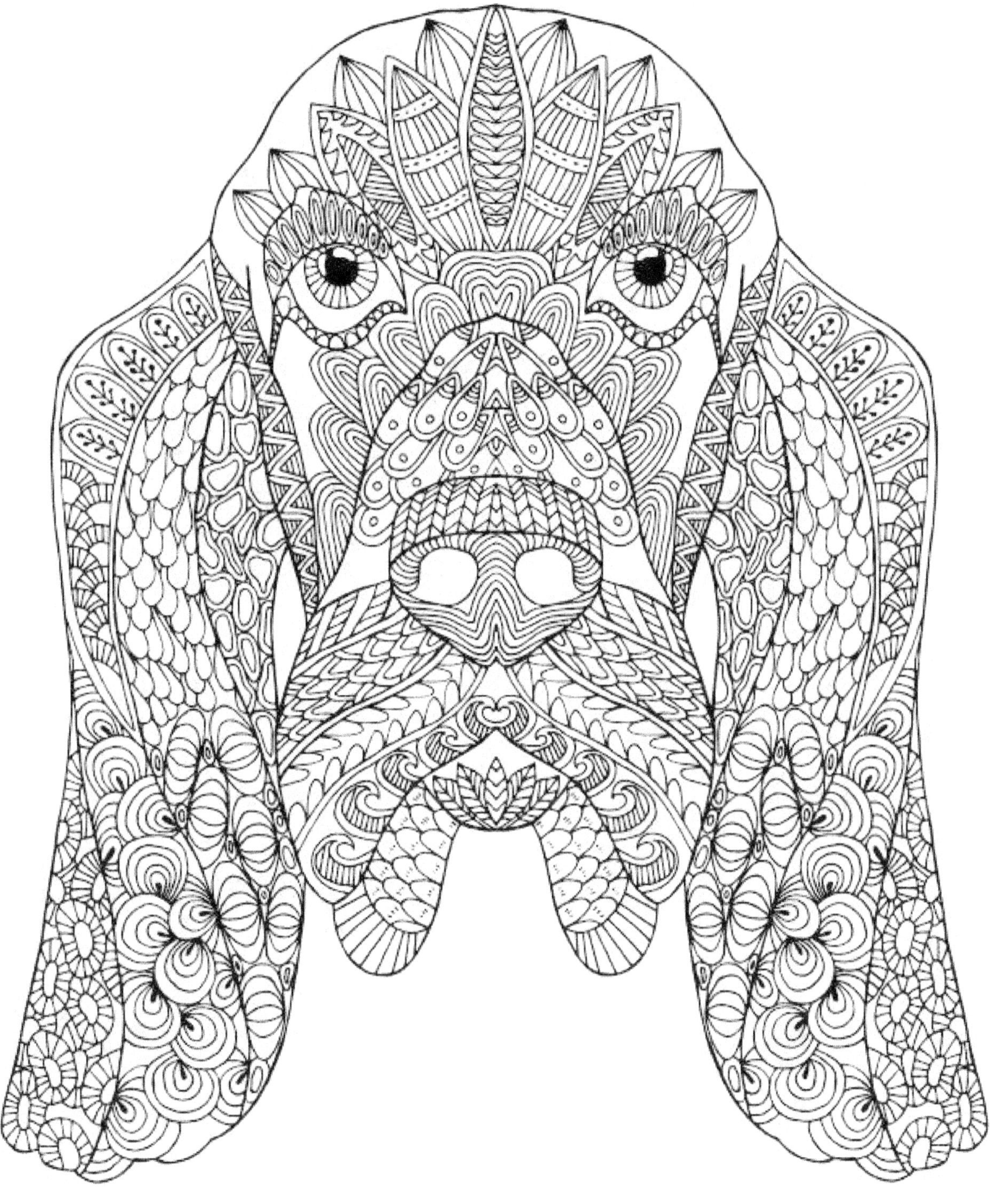

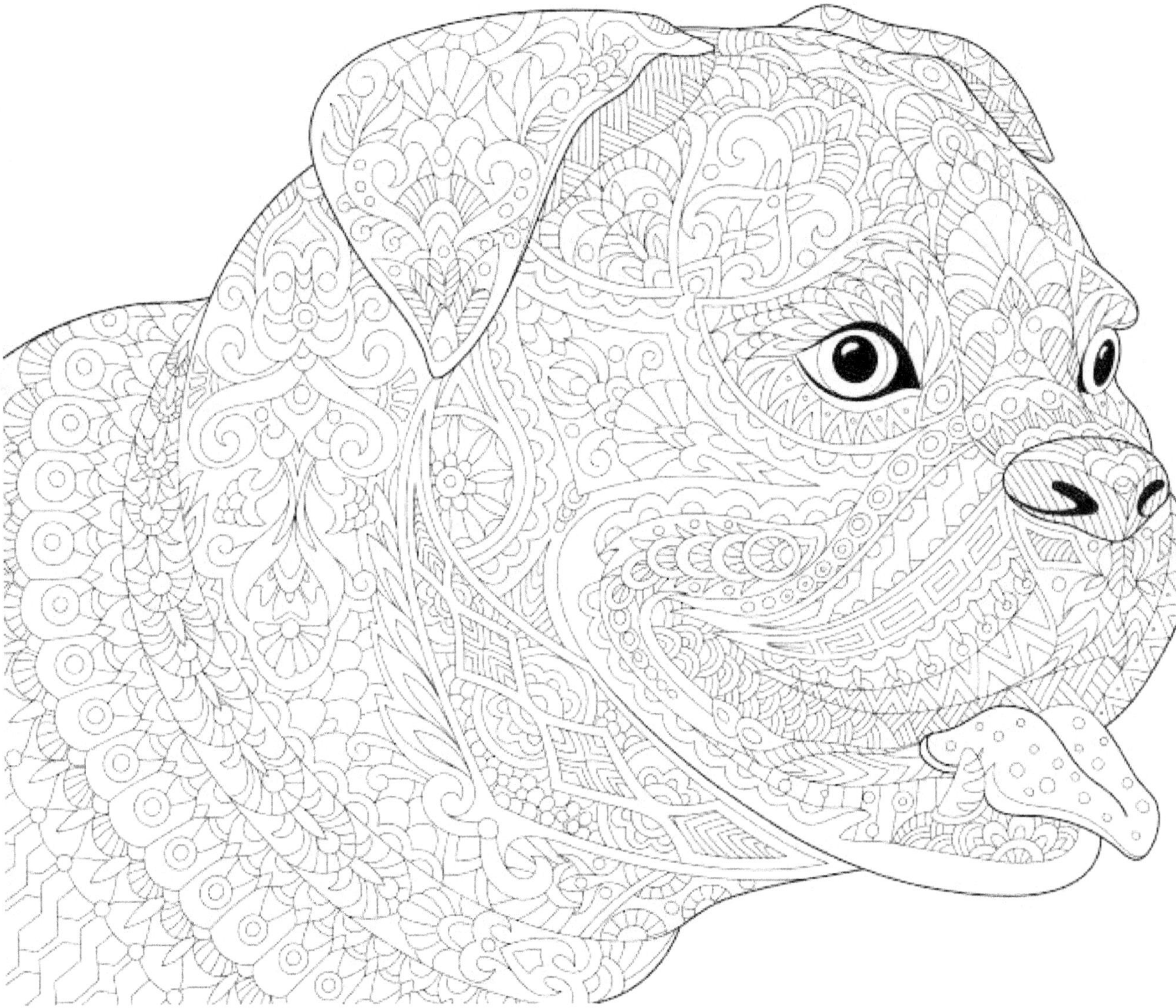

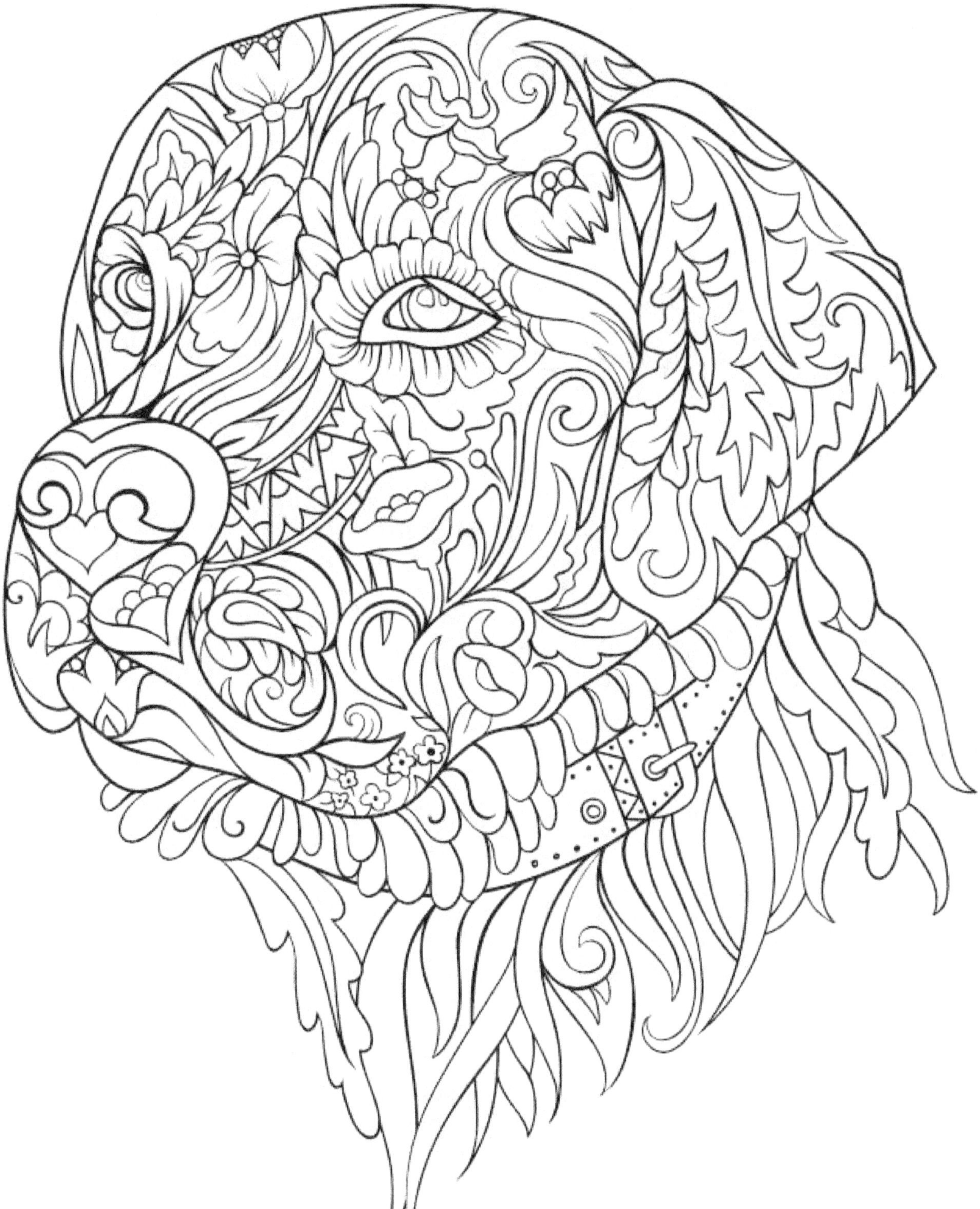

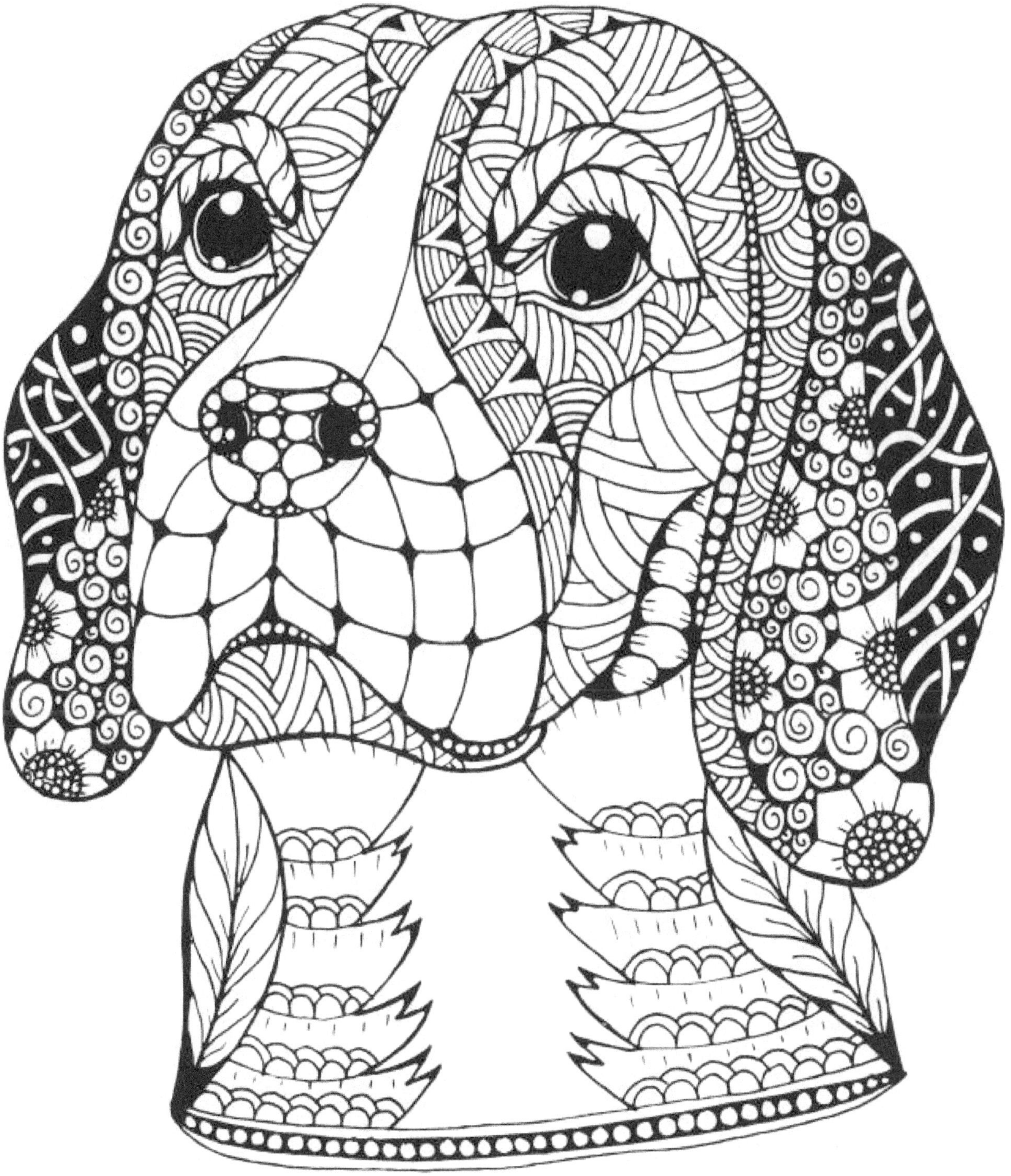

Surprise Bonus Sea Turtles Coloring Pages!

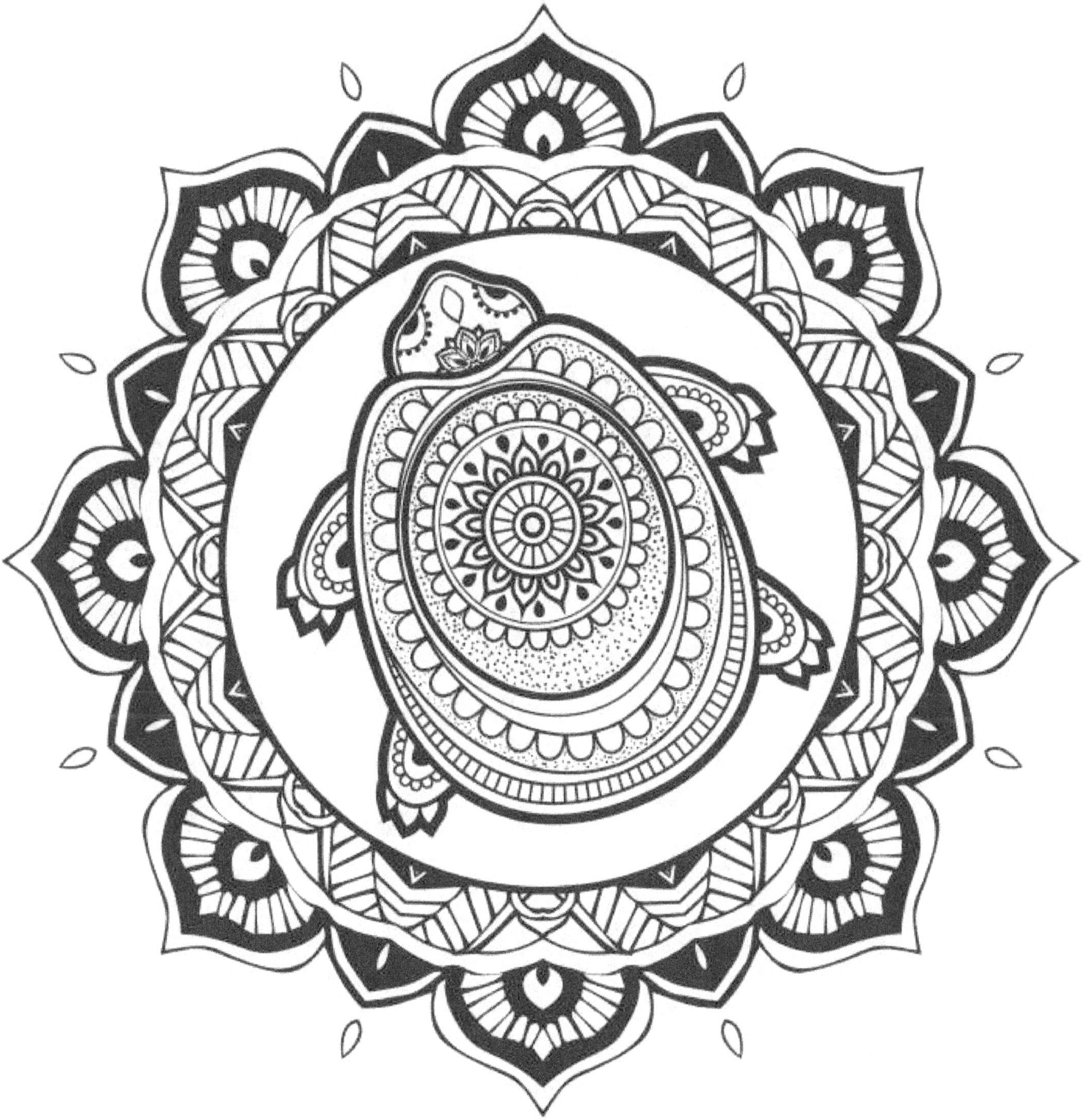

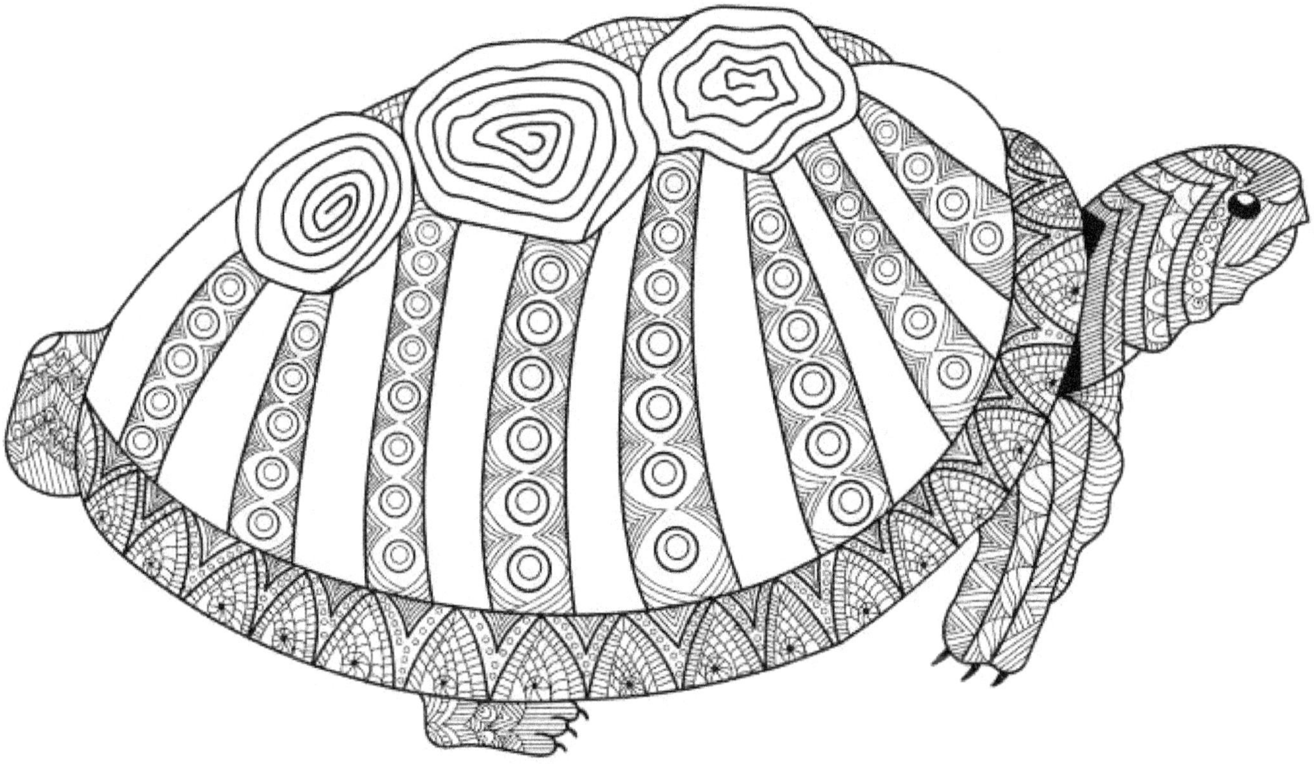

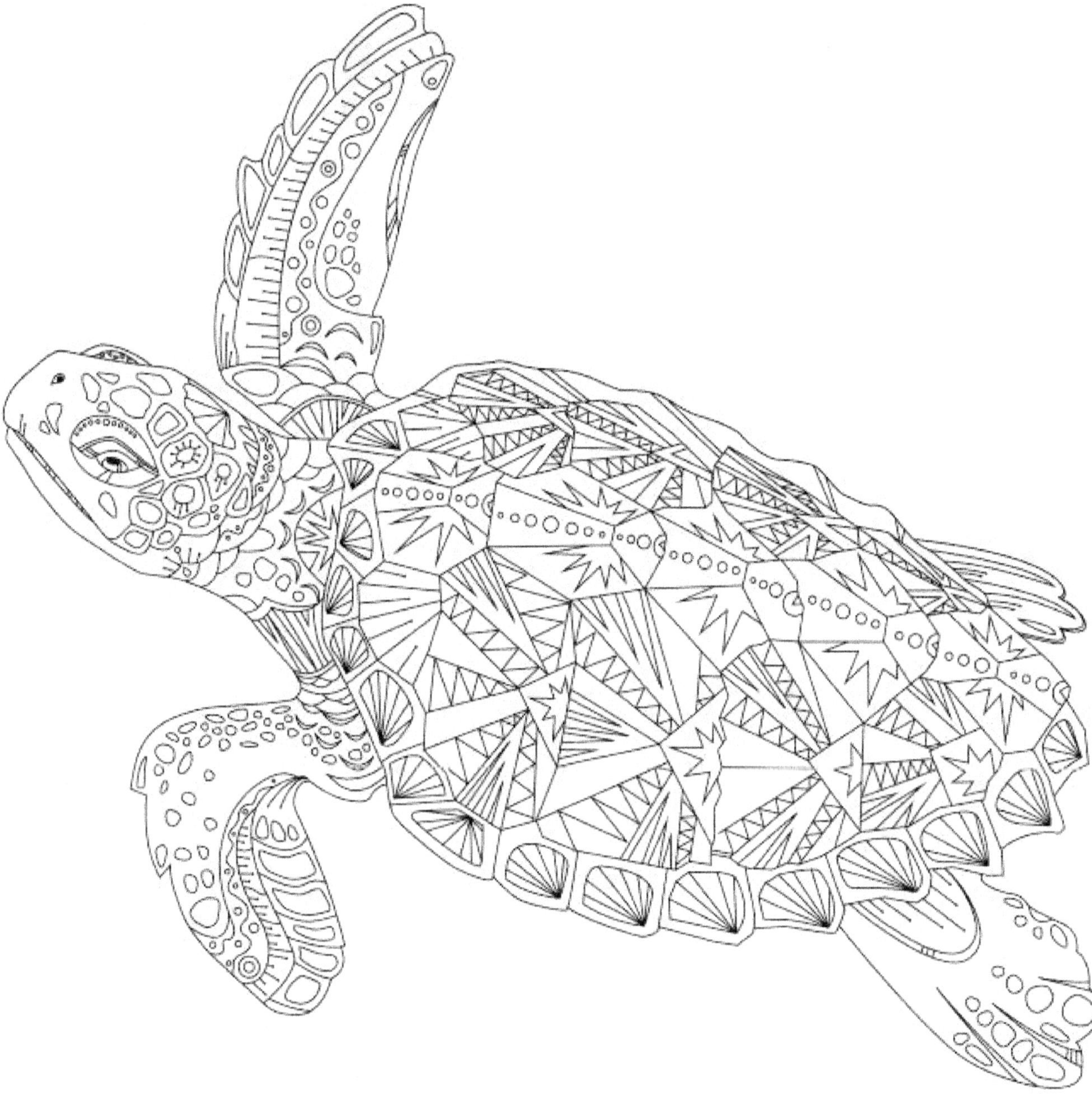

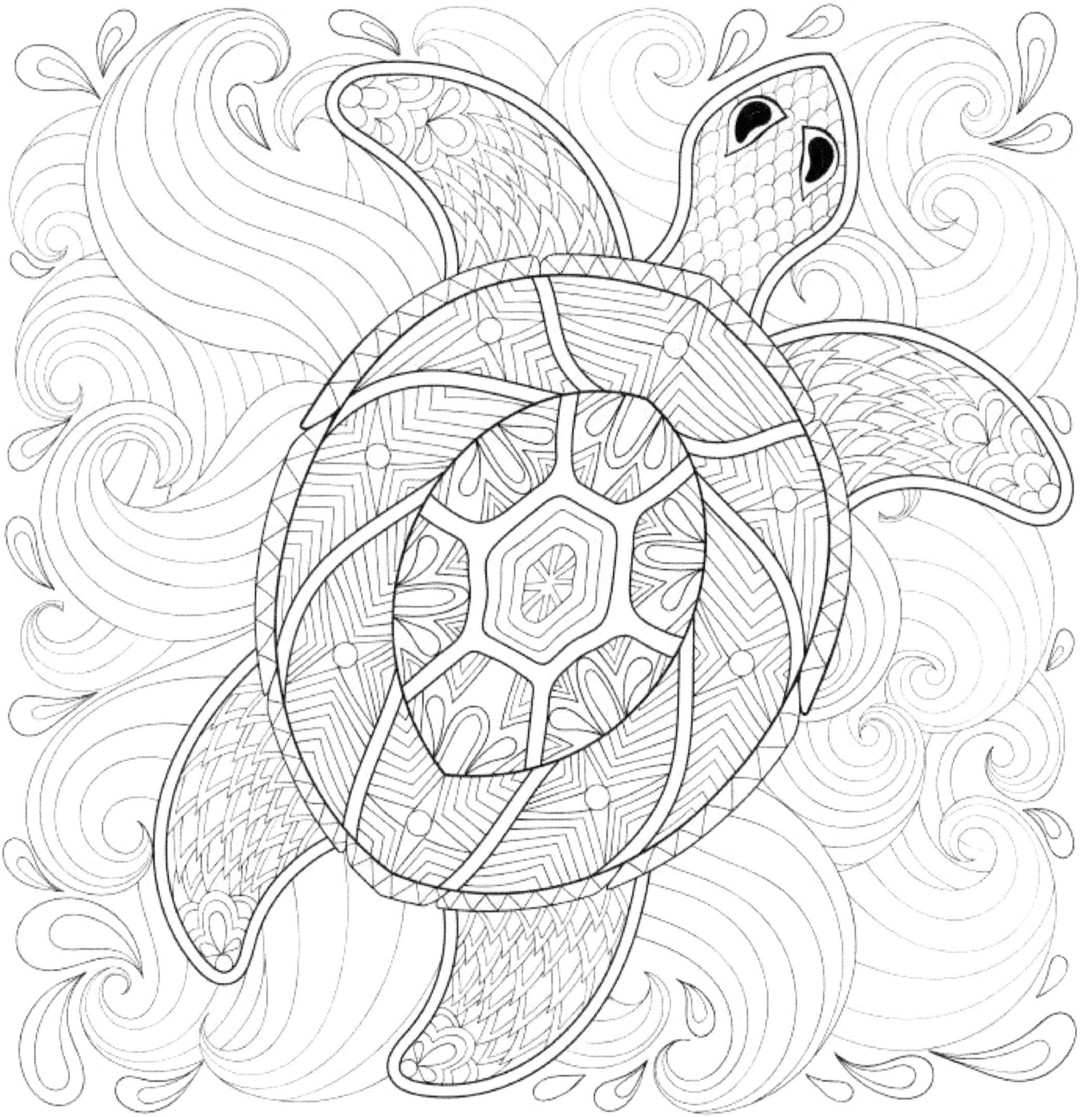

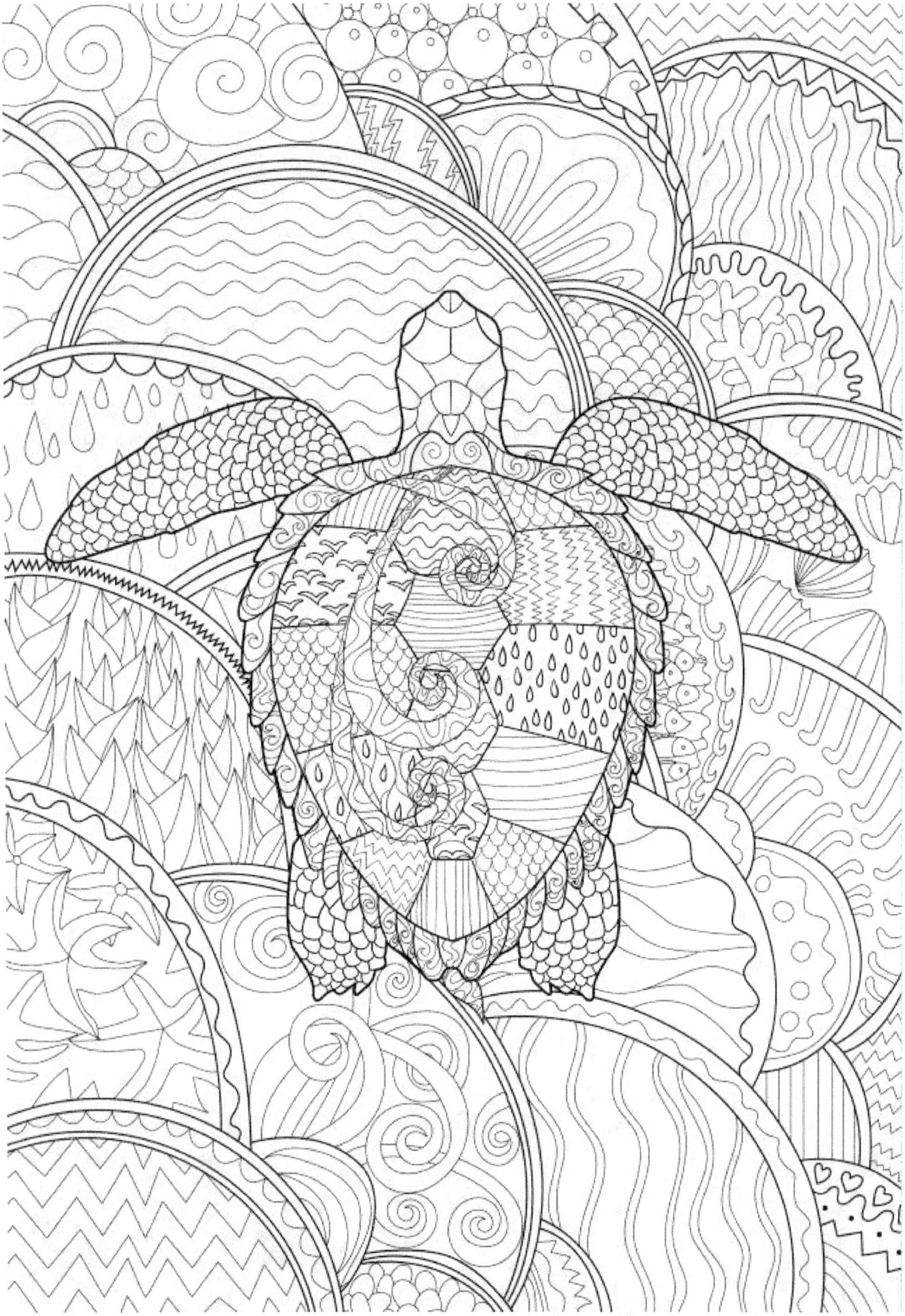

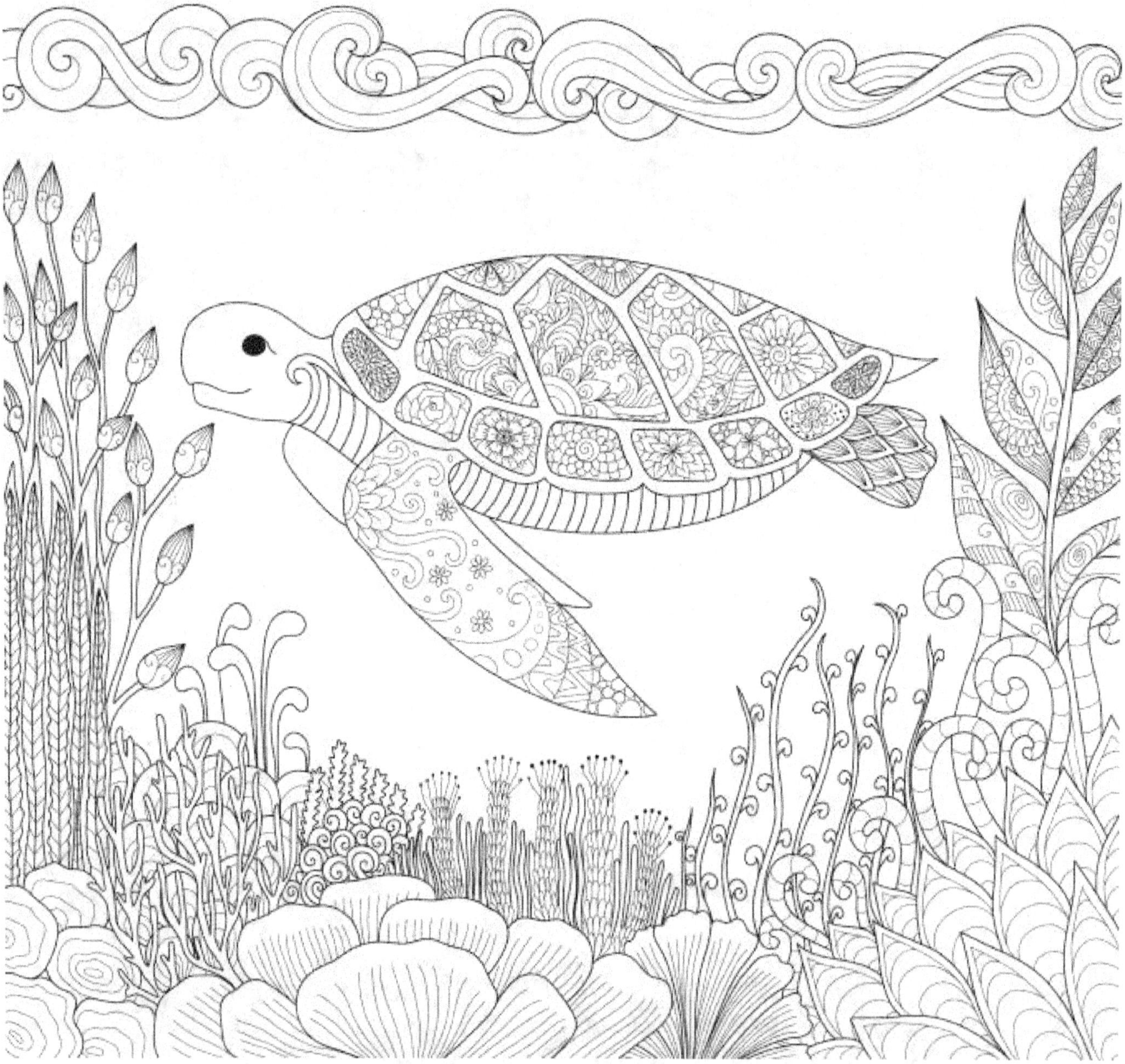

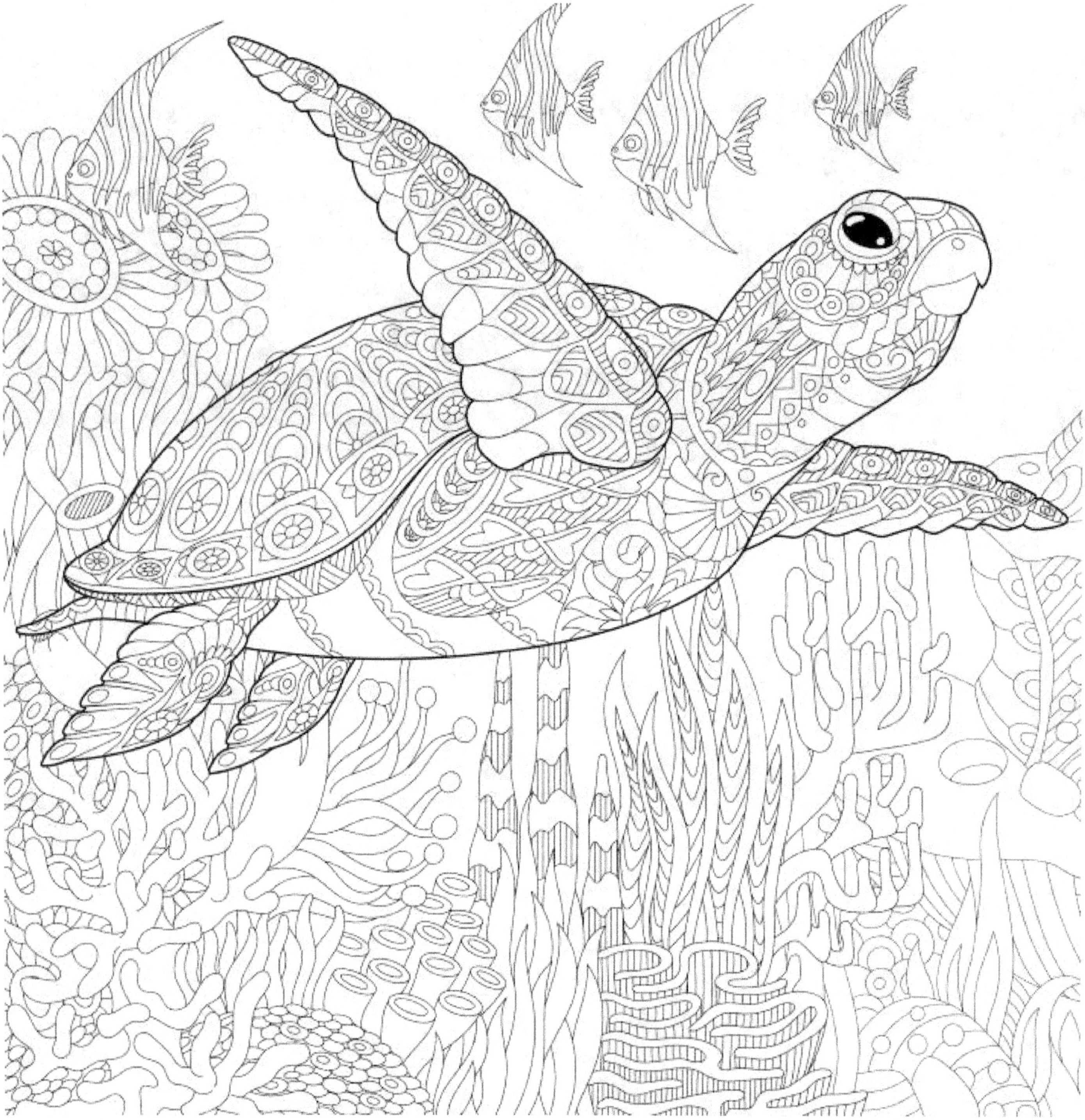

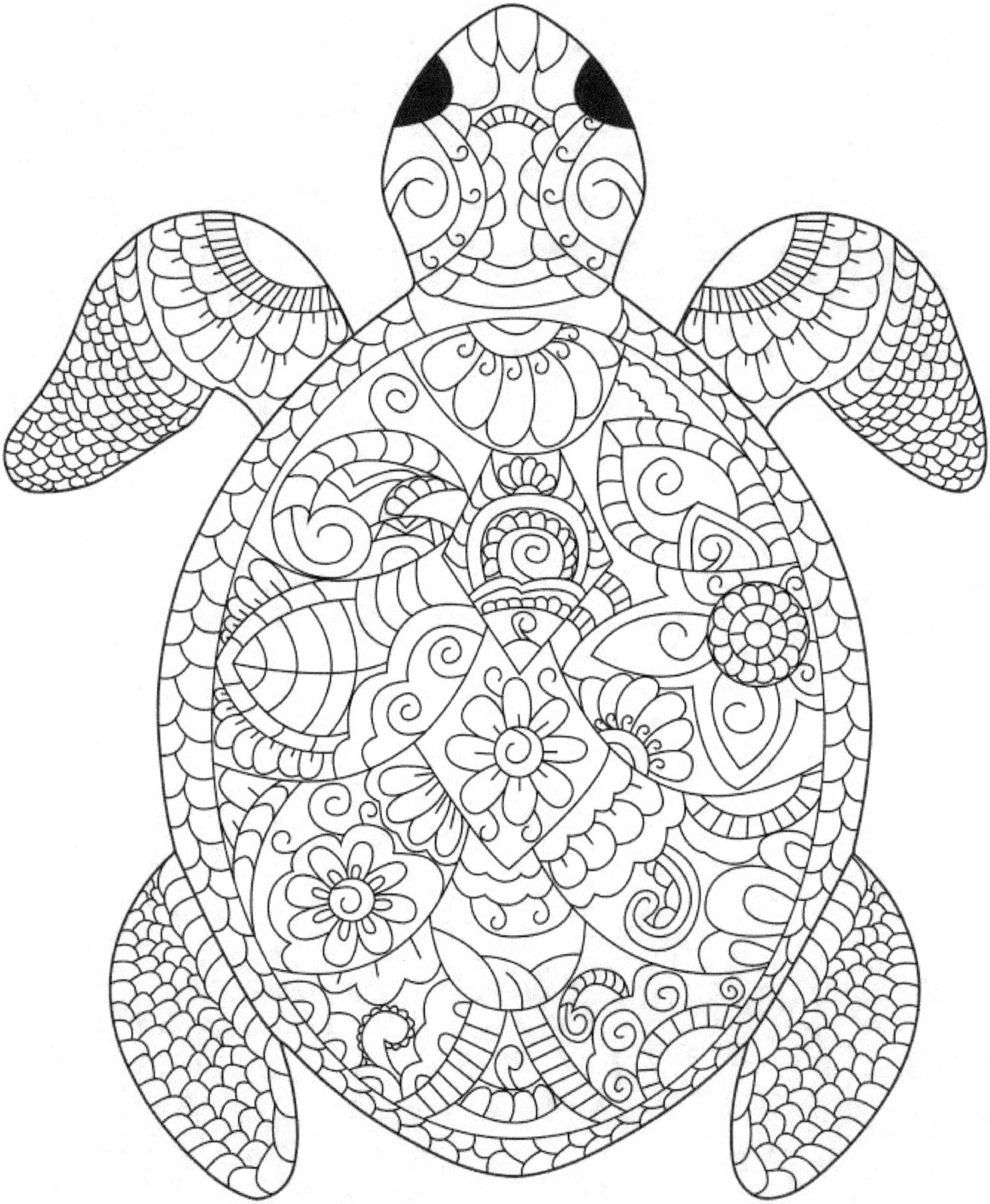

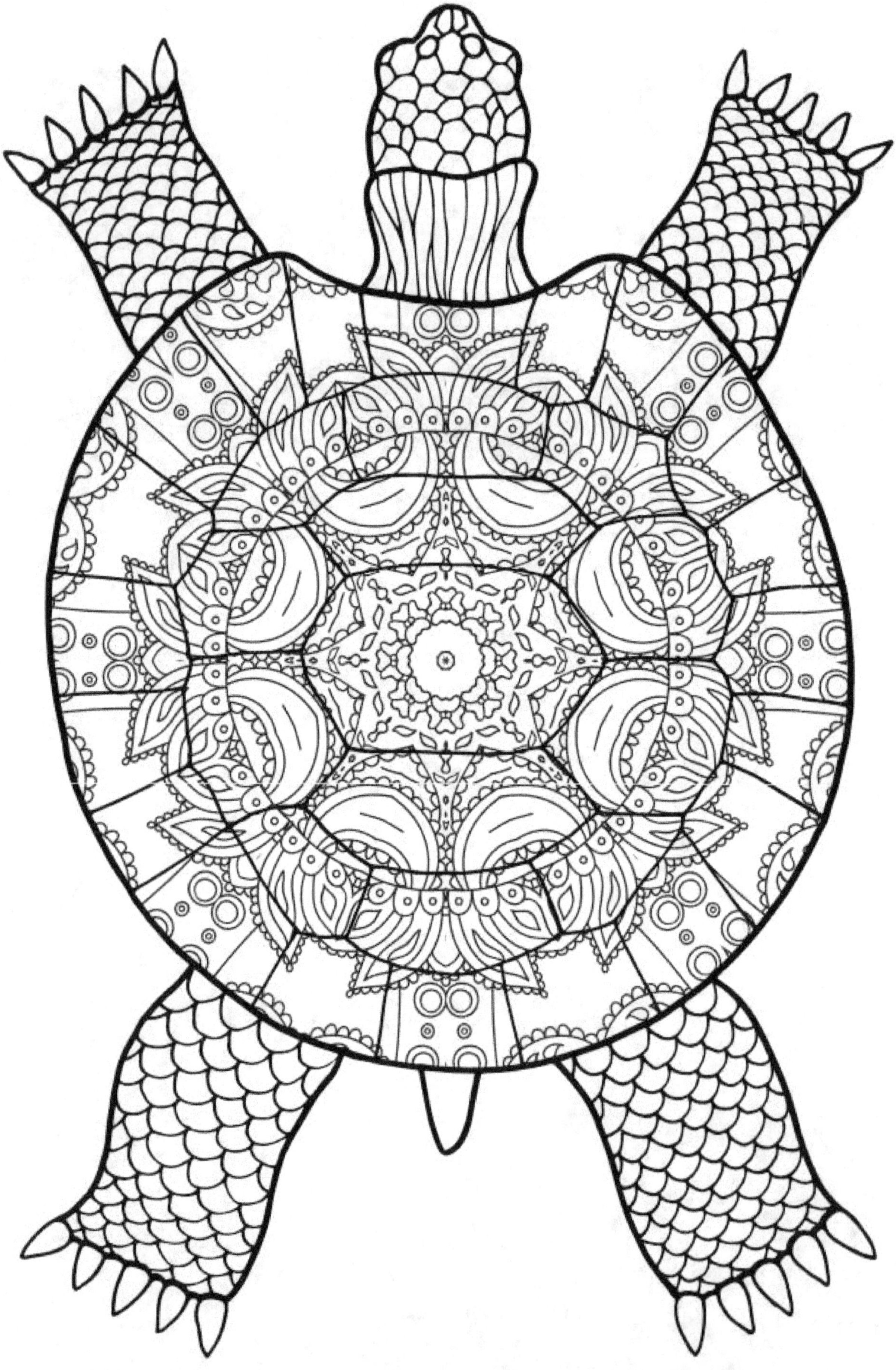

www.ingramcontent.com/pod-product-compliance
Lightning Source LLC
Chambersburg PA
CBHW081256180526
45170CB00007B/2453
* 9 7 8 1 5 4 6 8 3 3 5 5 0 *